Wanderer at the World's Edge

Poems by
Eugene O'Connor

BLUE LIGHT PRESS ✧ 1st WORLD PUBLISHING

1st WORLD
PUBLISHING

SAN FRANCISCO ✧ FAIRFIELD ✧ DELHI

2021 Blue Light Poetry Prize Finalist
Wanderer at the World's Edge

Copyright ©2022 Eugene O'Connor

BLUE LIGHT PRESS
www.bluelightpress.com
bluelightpress@aol.com

1ST WORLD PUBLISHING
PO Box 2211
Fairfield, IA 52556
www.1stworldpublishing.com

BOOK & COVER DESIGN
Melanie Gendron
melaniegendron999@gmail.com

COVER PHOTO
Melanie Gendron

AUTHOR PHOTO
Walker Photography

FIRST EDITION

ISBN: 978-1-4218-3719-2

In loving memory of my mother,
MARY ELLEN O'CONNOR
(1922–2019)

Of all the paths you take in life,
make sure a few of them are dirt.

– John Muir

Contents

There Is Truth in Dirt 1

Each Morning, Early 2

Abandonment 3

I Mark Time 4

My Narcissus Self 5

In This Interval 6

Piebald 7

Courting the Moon 8

Dawn Light 9

Farther Out 10

The Wolf in the Tale 11

Letter 12

Soon 13

A Wall of Feathers 14

Jugglers and Riddles 15

Winter Turning 16

In My Mind's Eye 17

The Kalends of November 18

Ebb 19

Time Sifted through an Hourglass 20

Acknowledgments 23

About the Author 25

There Is Truth in Dirt

Along the daily path I take
through sand and stunted grass
each morning and each afternoon

I look ahead and down
for colored stones, glass bits and shells
washed up abandoned by the sea –

the sea my banishment, its vast circle
surrounding this tiny island
at world's end,

where I raise an altar to unheeding gods
with a humble offering
of kelp laid out in strips.

Picked clean of shells and stones,
reminding me of all I've lost, my world
worn down to crumbs of sand and soil.

There is truth in dirt:
it tells me everything.

Each Morning, Early

Each morning, early,
a stroll, a walk along the shore.

The running world rolls open.
Day brightens on the water.

A lamp here and there
 casts a small pool of its own.

I must learn to be content
with these ambits of light,

content with this,
to wander at the world's edge,

my sin   my roaming life.

Abandonment

I sailed across the strait
and landed here, an exile.

Caesar's face, meanwhile, ornaments
his eagles, his gold sovereigns,
and the breastplates on his shining statues.

Odd bits these, here, of the "new order"
he's created: "Rome once brick, now marble,"
scratched on mud temple and latrine walls –

ballsy and articulate, as he is,
especially now, his enemies
buried or scuttled – like me.

In early morning fog
I conjure that city, now far distant,
beneath whose colonnades booths have been set up
for trade   for love.

I Mark Time

I mark time, like a clock,
a clock without hands.
Every minute, every second
my *now*, my *forever*.

Is this still part of that empire
He controls, or another world
entirely with its own weather,
planets, moon and stars?

The emperor is entitled
to ignore me, distant,
beyond time's measure. Such is
the Dear Leader's privilege.

O Rome, mistress of the world,
so hateful, so imperious. Still,
Ausonia's air, the magic of alien skies
haunt my dreams.

My Narcissus Self

Too long blind to anything
but my own reflection
in admiring eyes,

I became one
with placid pools.

The river of complexity
that runs through every life
too turbid for my sailing –

thick waves and whitecaps rushing
toward a sudden waterfall.

And so I fell, feckless helmsman,
my shallow skiff shredded
on jagged rocks.

A ruin now, not fit
to court myself, no longer welcome
to a lover's gaze,
I'm no match for any weather,

but a wrack of my old self,
a painted rag upon a broken stick.

In This Interval

In the early morning dark
I pace back and forth and think
about my age now, with
its ills and discontents:

the pain in my left side
that doesn't go away
and drives off sleep,

grief bubbling up
as memories flow through –
dark spirit breaths.
I make room for them

in this interval –

That this sounds poetic
is incidental.
It is knowledge first –
It is what I need to stay alive.

I know
that in that far-off Capital
people cheer and wave
as Caesar rides past
in his victory car:

the horses' tentative gallop,
their sudden bolt.

Piebald

Gratitude now for piebald things:
the runt horse dappled in black and white
as it stands in the cold paddock,
trees gaunt and empty, their branches tossed
by winter winds.

Over the dark earth skitter faded leaves,
the wing of a dead bird, its feathers ruffled,
simulates flight.
Traces of calcite, a long stretch of mottled wall.

But hope fades with evening coming on
and promises of snow. Bracing night air
will scrub and polish surfaces that jut
above the frozen soil.

This, my burial place – black and white,
these scarred stones my headstone
with no epitaph, no formulae of praise,
not even dates of birth and death.

My only monument this angular terrain
silhouetted by the moon and stars.

Courting the Moon

I used to watch the moon
track her long path through the sky
as she gathered stars

and cast them down like torches
on the ocean's briny surface –
a momentary hiss and sparkle.

Once I had the power to draw
the bright moon down, to kiss
her mottled cheek.

Once I had the power to reverse
the course of running streams.
I strode the long stretch of the sea.

I have no power now, no longer
even to traverse this narrow island cell
of rocks and gritty sand.

The stars grow alien, the moon
conceals her glow, although she
once let me lift the crescent

from her brow and loosen her long hair
to wash it in a cerulean bowl.

Dawn Light

Dawn follows a night
of such grief, such grave disorder.
It is the light – or lack of it –
that drives me inward, away
from the sun that, when it comes,
scorches and blinds.

It is felt even by the leafless trees
scraping their brittle branches together
following a long night

of suffering that blooms and blisters
like stale fruit, bitter to taste,
even more bitter to swallow.

I swallow gales. I swallow grief
that weighs me down
in cold that makes
the barren trees explode.

Farther Out

The trees have changed and even in
their leaflessness have softened
as has the blue sky overhead.

There are no clouds to speak
of trouble up ahead,

though snowfall is expected to come soon,
with early darkness.

Farther out lies more unsteady quiet.
Farther out there are more sober plans.

The past remains
a deeply scarred country.

Call it the pattern of the weather.

The Wolf in the Tale

I steal along beneath
the moon's dim glow.

I speak in voice so low
my few words rustle
like dry leaves.

Were I a bird,
I would utter prophecies.

Low light belongs to me.
I wear it like a mask
of evening.

My footprints
all that's visible
in the leaves I crushed –

those same leaves I whisper to
in my dark fury,
furred like an animal

roaming in shadows
black as winter trees,
gray as the torn coat
left forgotten where it fell.

Letter

The only letter left
from the Great Struggle
is the one I wrote myself –
myself to me:

epic-length, long drawn out
in which I brandished my medals,
absolved myself of blame

for my relegation –
to Pontus, to Crimea, Siberia,
lands of frozen waste

where I strain rennet through a sieve
and pack mendacity in jars.

Why speak of her for whose love
two nights melted into one?

What's to be gained
by going on and on in such
a tedious self-defense?

Can a mere mortal fight
against a god-man and win –
even a god-man whose splendor
is fraudulent?

Soon

Soon, someday soon, I will do it,
toss fistfuls of grass over the ice
to melt it.

No more skating
on the pond. It is rendered
liquid and unusable.

The ice already cracked,
I look down to see
my features pinch and wrinkle.

From far off I hear a voice,
the sound of rain.

My eyes, a bird's eyes, dart back
and forth, urgency's call
to attention.

Words fly to me, at last –
softly feathered, kind.
The water flows.

A Wall of Feathers

Is this now the part I play?
Is mine the role of beak
and open throat?

My chest a wall of feathers,
I'm poised for flight,
to sing at dawn,

songs of earth,
its moss and lichen –

a nest of chicks
bundled in a bed of leaves,

turning into birds
as all earth's women used to do,
nurturers high up there,
eager for their chicks to fly,
to be gone.

Avoiding songs of healing,
shunning immortality, I stand
for brood and branch,
each momentary feather

drifting softly
as the wing it left.

Jugglers and Riddles

The edges of the world
cannot be far away.
I test its borders as it moves.

I turn with the earthly gods.
I have been doing this forever.

I shuffle dry leaves
from Dodonean oaks to read
like pages in a book

and carve fresh riddles
on the skin of trees.

Winter Turning

Gray sky, a thin snow coats
the grass and bare tree branches.
In the fallow field nothing stirs
beyond the stream's swift glide
over rocks, tempered, then slowed
to a crawl before freezing fast.

The solstice festival two weeks off,
though mine will steal in quietly
and as quiet go, as December scutters off
without the usual noise of celebration.

Instead, the neighboring cowherd
will prepare to rise at three to attend
the calf's birth, spreading fresh hay
for the new life coming in wet, steaming
with its first raw breaths.

First light comes, and with it
a sharp breeze. The branches shift
and drifts of fresh snow settle as,
birthing done, the mother lows
and licks her young and eats
the afterbirth.

I watch as those men – weary, grateful –
lumber slowly out of doors. I long
to wander with them, their human warmth –

the feel of your hand, my hand

In My Mind's Eye

I see in my mind's eye
the sights denied to me
by distance, by the fact of exile.

Though a curtain of snow falls
and your voice grows faint
as someone saying, ruefully:
Goodbye,

I'll pluck each word
out of your open mouth,
each time pleading:

Tell me something good.

The Kalends of November

*– with the last two lines adapted from Roger Reeves's poem
"Tiresias, at the End of the World"*

In this same place,
in my "winter palace,"

last evening's clocks
slept on tufted pillows

as the world turned
to deeper dusk and dark.

Now and forever a wanderer,
let me take pleasure where I can

and be grateful
for small grains of light

and find another language of remorse –
try silence, even,

when words themselves
will not avail.

In silence allow me
to express my praise

hidden in degrees of darkness
pricked with stars –

glossy silver threads
in a broad tapestry.

No region of night's exile
is without its ecstasy.

Ebb

As daylight shrinks bright colors
slip away with one final gleam
of pink and rose and grow one
with the horizon.

My thoughts meander to the border
of the page this world is written on,
the earth and sky that watches me,
each new star an eye, every shore light
a beacon

by which I saw that man's body
rolling in to shore, limbs splayed,
then settled in the still warm sand
and, judging by his clothes,
an indigent.

Or was that the work of salt,
of storms offshore, their churning toil
and forked lightning?

I am bound to the edge,
I crave firm ground, even as
the night sky revolves above me.

The earth and all its stars move regular
as clocks. Regular as clocks the dead
roll in, in rags or cloth of gold,
in search of fertile soil.

I'll bury them obligingly, stacking them
like bricks in common graves,
or rake them into heaps
like autumn leaves.

Time Sifted through an Hourglass

The dirt across my path
I consult once more, like sand sifted
through an hourglass.

Endless hours I turn the glass over
and start again.
I juggle conjuring stones.

I plant fresh prophecies in soil
and carve new poems
on the bark of trees.

There, in the arc,
the beauty of a line.

Acknowledgments

The Avocet: "Piebald"
Pudding Magazine: "Farther Out"

About the Author

Eugene O'Connor's poetry and translations have appeared in *arlington literary journal, The Avocet, Classical Bulletin, Classical Outlook, Common Threads, The Comstock Review, The Columbia Anthology of Gay Literature, Mead, OASIS Journal, Poetry Pacific, Pudding Magazine, Roman Poets of the Early Empire* (Penguin), and elsewhere. His two previous chapbooks are *Derelict Mansions* (2011) and *The Same Sea, the Same Gloaming* (2018). A native of Buffalo, New York, he holds a BA in Latin from Canisius College, an MA in Comparative Literature from the University of Rochester, and a Ph.D. in Classics from The University of California, Santa Barbara. His English translation, with notes and introduction, of Renaissance humanist Antonio Beccadelli's *Hermaphroditus* was published by Lexington Books in 2001.

Eugene O'Connor lives with his husband in Columbus, Ohio.

www.ingramcontent.com/pod-product-compliance
Lightning Source LLC
Chambersburg PA
CBHW021917040426
42447CB00007B/907